S0-BCR-347

The Montgomery
Bus Boycott

Sabrina Crewe and Frank Walsh

Gareth Stevens Publishing

A WORLD ALMANAC EDUCATION GROUP COMPANY

Please visit our web site at: www.garethstevens.com
For a free color catalog describing Gareth Stevens Publishing's list of high-quality
books and multimedia programs, call 1-800-542-2595 (USA) or 1-800-387-3178
(Canada). Gareth Stevens Publishing's fax: (414) 332-3567.

Library of Congress Cataloging-in-Publication Data

Crewe, Sabrina.
 The Montgomery bus boycott / by Sabrina Crewe and Frank Walsh.
  p. cm. — (Events that shaped America)
 Includes bibliographical references and index.
 ISBN 0-8368-3394-5 (lib. bdg.)
 1. Montgomery (Ala.)—Race relations—Juvenile literature. 2. Segregation in
transportation—Alabama—Montgomery—History—20th century—Juvenile literature.
3. African Americans—Civil rights—Alabama—Montgomery—History—20th century—
Juvenile literature. [1. Montgomery (Ala.)—Race relations. 2. Segregation in
transportation—History. 3. African Americans—Civil rights.] I. Walsh, Frank.
II. Title. III. Series.
 F334.M79N427 2003
 323.1'196073076147—dc21   2002030993

First published in 2003 by
Gareth Stevens Publishing
A World Almanac Education Group Company
330 West Olive Street, Suite 100
Milwaukee, WI 53212 USA

Copyright © 2003 by Gareth Stevens Publishing.

Produced by Discovery Books
Editor: Sabrina Crewe
Designer and page production: Sabine Beaupré
Photo researcher: Sabrina Crewe
Maps and diagrams: Stefan Chabluk
Gareth Stevens editorial direction: Mark J. Sachner
Gareth Stevens art direction: Tammy Gruenewald
Gareth Stevens production: Jessica Yanke

Photo credits: Corbis: cover, pp. 4, 5, 6, 7 (both), 9, 10, 11, 12, 13, 15, 16, 20, 22, 24, 26;
Henry Ford Museum and Greenfield Village: pp. 14, 18, 27; Library of Congress:
pp. 17, 21, 23, 25; Rosa Parks Museum and Library, Troy State University: p. 19.

All rights reserved. No part of this book may be reproduced, stored in a retrieval system,
or transmitted in any form or by any means, electronic, mechanical, photocopying,
recording, or otherwise, without the prior written permission of the copyright holder.

Printed in the United States of America

1 2 3 4 5 6 7 8 9 07 06 05 04 03

Contents

Introduction

A sculpture of Rosa Parks is displayed in the Civil Rights Institute in Birmingham, Alabama. It celebrates Parks's historic journey on December 1, 1955.

Tired of Being Trampled

"There comes a time when people get tired of being trampled over by the iron feet of **oppression**. . . . I want it to be known that we're going to work with grim and bold determination to gain justice on buses in this city. And we are not wrong. . . . If we are wrong, justice is a lie."

Martin Luther King, Jr.,
Montgomery, Alabama,
December 5, 1955

Montgomery, 1955

About fifty years ago, Montgomery, Alabama, was the location of a very important event. At first, nobody knew how important it would turn out to be.

This is what happened. On December 1, 1955, a black woman named Rosa Parks refused the order of a bus driver to give up her seat to a white passenger on a Montgomery public bus. Parks was arrested because she had defied not just the rules of the bus company but the **segregation** laws in Alabama.

African Americans in Montgomery were tired of segregation and of being humiliated by bus drivers. They organized a **boycott** to protest Parks's arrest. This meant that, for over a year, all African Americans refused to use the Montgomery bus system. The boycott ended only when segregation on buses was declared **unconstitutional**.

Civil Rights

Americans had been fighting segregation for some time. But the Montgomery bus boycott was important because it was the start of a movement in the 1950s and 1960s that finally succeeded in gaining **civil rights** for all U.S. citizens. The story of the boycott continues to inspire people who are fighting inequality in society today.

The City of Montgomery

Montgomery, capital of Alabama, is located in the center of the state and covers an area of about 135 square miles (350 square kilometers). In the year 2000, the population of Montgomery was just over 220,000.

The State Capitol building in Montgomery.

Montgomery is famous for a number of reasons, including being the site of the first electric streetcar system established in 1886. The Wright Brothers founded the first civilian flying school there in 1910. Montgomery is also the site chosen for Air University—the education arm of the Air Force—that opened in 1946.

Chapter One

Slavery in America

Slaves were property, just like furniture or cattle. Every year in Montgomery, an auction was held where white people could buy and sell slaves. This drawing shows that auction in 1861.

How Slavery Began

In 1619, a Dutch trader brought a small group of Africans to Virginia. He handed over the Africans to colonists there in exchange for food. This was the first time that Africans were brought to America and sold as slaves.

In 1641, Massachusetts became the first colony to make slavery official. One by one, the other colonies continued this process until Georgia, the last free colony, legalized slavery in 1750. Slavery was a fact of life in the United States from the moment the country declared its independence in 1776. Even Thomas Jefferson—who wrote in the Declaration of Independence that "all men are created equal"—kept slaves.

A Life of Slavery

Slavery became essential to the U.S. **economy**, particularly in the southern states, or "the South." Most slaves farmed cotton, tobacco, and other crops on southern plantations, which were large farms that depended on slave labor. Many slaves lived and worked in terrible conditions and were punished with beatings. Slaves were property, and they were expected to live without any of the rights or dignity of free people.

The Abolitionists

There were people in the 1700s and 1800s who fought for the civil rights of slaves in America. They were known as "abolitionists" because they wanted to **abolish** slavery.

William Lloyd Garrison (1805–1879) published and edited a newspaper called the *Liberator*. He was frequently attacked by white people in the North and the South for what he wrote. Sojourner Truth (1797–1883) was a former slave who became a Christian preacher and then a lecturer for the abolitionist cause. After the **Civil War**, Truth worked to help freed slaves in Virginia and Washington, D.C. Frederick Douglass (1817–1896) escaped from slavery in 1838. He was a great speaker for the abolitionist movement. After the Civil War, Douglass worked for the U.S. government both in Washington, D.C., and in the Caribbean.

Sojourner Truth

Frederick Douglass

KEY
- Union states
- Confederate states
- Border states (Union)
- United States territories

This map shows the United States and Confederate States during the Civil War. Border states allowed slavery but stayed loyal to the Union. For a while, Montgomery was the Confederacy's capital.

The Split Between North and South

By the early 1800s, slavery had been abolished in nearly all northern states. In the South, however, there were more than 3.5 million slaves by 1860. Northerners were speaking out more and more against slavery, and southern slave owners were afraid that abolitionists would take away their right to keep slaves.

Bad feeling grew between North and South in the 1840s and 1850s. The breaking point came in 1860, when Abraham Lincoln was elected president. Lincoln belonged to the new Republican Party, which opposed the spread of slavery.

The Civil War Ends Slavery

In 1861, eleven southern states formed a new nation with its own government called the Confederate States of America. The North and the South could find no way to resolve their differences, and the two sides went to war in the Civil War, which began on April 12, 1861.

8

The End of Slavery

"We shout for joy that we live to recall this righteous moment. . . . . 'Free forever' oh! Long enslaved millions, . . . the hour of your deliverance draws nigh! . . . Ye millions of free and loyal men . . . lift up your voices with joy and thanksgiving for with freedom to the slave will come peace and safety to your country."

*Frederick Douglass, abolitionist, speaking
about the abolition of slavery*

On January 1, 1863, President Lincoln abolished slavery in the South with the **Emancipation** Proclamation. But the South ignored the proclamation, and slavery continued in the Confederate states. It was four long and bloody years before the Confederacy surrendered on April 9, 1865, and the Civil War was over. In December 1865, slavery was officially banned in the United States by the Thirteenth **Amendment** to the U.S. Constitution.

A painting celebrates the end of slavery by showing Lincoln, on horseback, holding the Emancipation Proclamation. The woman in the carriage is a symbol of freedom.

Chapter Two

Segregation and Racism

Racist Laws

Although some people worked to gain civil rights for the newly freed slaves, others tried to keep black people in a state of poverty and oppression. This was because so many white Americans were **racist**. They continued to believe whites were superior to black people.

Over the years, the Southern states managed to erode the few rights gained by African Americans after the Civil War. They stopped blacks from voting by coming up with new laws. For instance, these laws would say that people had to read and write or own property before they could vote. Most blacks did not qualify, and so they were barred from voting.

After slavery was abolished, some white people made sure black people did not achieve equality. They used violence to punish black people for even the smallest offense.

Jim Crow

By the 1890s, a society based on slavery had turned into one based on segregation. Laws and white attitudes in the South made it impossible for black people to gain the basic rights or opportunities that would give them equality. Segregation laws were known as "Jim Crow" laws. They got this name from a character invented by a white entertainer to make fun of black people.

Life Under Segregation

In 1896, the **Supreme Court** ruled that segregation of races was acceptable as long as "separate but equal" public facilities were available for blacks. This ruling meant that segregation would last for many years to come. But the facilities were like the society that provided them, and they were hardly ever equal. Black people got the

A segregated drinking fountain in the South.

worst seats in theaters and bad service in restaurants. They had few resources for their schools and received no respect from business owners and officials. They could not choose where they worked or what neighborhood they lived in.

Every day, African Americans were attacked and threatened by white people. They would be punished for actions as innocent as looking a white person in the eye or not being humble enough in some other way. If blacks physically defended themselves against violence, however, they could be killed.

Thurgood Marshall, center, stands outside the Supreme Court after his victory in *Brown v. Board of Education*. In 1967, Marshall became the first black justice appointed to the Supreme Court.

The Supreme Court Decision

"We conclude that in the field of public education the doctrine of 'separate but equal' has no place. Separate educational facilities are . . . unequal."

U.S. Supreme Court, Brown v. Board of Education, *1954*

The Beginning of Change

On February 12, 1909, the National Association for the Advancement of Colored People (NAACP) was founded by a group of **activists**. The NAACP began many years of fighting for change. In one of their most famous court cases, *Brown v. Board of Education of Topeka*, the NAACP fought in the Supreme Court for Linda Brown, an African American barred from her neighborhood school because of segregation.

The Supreme Court trial began in December 1852 and continued until May 17, 1954. The Supreme Court said that its earlier "separate but equal" ruling was unconstitutional and that segregation in schools was wrong. It was a major victory in the struggle for civil rights. Slowly, a change was beginning to take place in the South.

Resistance to Equality

After the *Brown v. Board of Education* verdict, however, there was a new sense of danger in the South. The Supreme Court's ruling angered many white people. Only two southern states, Texas and Arkansas, began **desegregation** in 1954. Across the South, whites continued to resist equal rights for blacks.

The Murder of Emmett Till

Racial hatred in the South led to the murder of a fourteen-year-old African-American boy named Emmett Till. Emmett was visiting some of his relatives in Money, Mississippi, from his home in Chicago in August 1955, when he broke the rules of racism. During his visit, Emmett was challenged by some local boys to speak to a white woman. He did. Three days later, Emmett was killed.

Mose Wright, with whom Emmett had been staying, testified against the two white men accused of the murder. It was one of the first times that a black man in the South had risked testifying against a white man. The men were not convicted, however, because the jury was all white. It would not convict white men of a crime against a black person.

Chapter Three

The Boycott

The bus yard of Montgomery City Bus Lines in the 1950s.

The Montgomery Bus System

Like most public facilities in Montgomery, the buses were segregated. The front of the bus was for whites only and the back of the bus was for black people. And if a bus became crowded, blacks were to give up their seats so that white people could sit down. All of the bus drivers were white.

December 1, 1955

On the evening of December 1, 1955, a tailor's assistant named Rosa Parks left her job at a Montgomery department store, walked to her bus stop, and boarded a crowded bus to ride home. At the next stop, even more passengers boarded. The driver, James Blake, ordered the blacks who were sitting to give up their seats for the white riders. Parks refused to move. Blake threatened to call the police and have Parks arrested. Parks replied, "You may do that."

Dignity and Self-Respect
"What I learned best at Miss White's school [Montgomery Industrial School for Girls] was that I was a person with dignity and self-respect, and I should not set my sights lower than anybody else just because I was black."

Rosa Parks, writing about her experience at the school for African-American girls she attended in 1924, Rosa Parks: My Story, *1992*

Rosa Parks at the ceremony awarding her the Congressional Gold Medal in 1999.

Rosa Parks was born in Tuskegee, Alabama, and she grew up in the small town of Pine Level near Montgomery. As small children, Rosa and her brother went to a segregated rural school. At eleven, years old, Rosa Parks entered the Montgomery Industrial School for Girls, and later she went on to the Booker T. Washington Junior High School. She left school before graduating to care for her family, but she graduated later.

In 1932, Rosa married a Montgomery barber named Raymond Parks, who was a member of the NAACP. She was soon actively involved in civil rights, and in 1943 she became secretary of the Montgomery branch of the NAACP.

After the Montgomery bus boycott ended, Rosa and Raymond Parks lost their jobs and were threatened with violence. The couple moved to Detroit, Michigan, where Rosa Parks worked for Congressman John Conyers until her retirement.

Planning the Boycott

Rosa Parks was arrested and taken to the city jail. Police took her picture and fingerprints and then released her. She was later convicted of violating segregation laws.

Edward D. Nixon was a NAACP leader who wanted to organize a protest against segregation. Rosa Parks was exactly the right kind of person he had been looking for to be a **figurehead** for the protest. He told Parks that, with her permission, they could use her case to break down segregation on the buses. Parks didn't have to think very long. She said, "I'll go along with you, Mr. Nixon." It was decided that there would be a boycott of the Montgomery bus system in support of Parks on Monday, December 5.

Edward D. Nixon, seen here with Rosa Parks, was a fighter against segregation. In 1955, he was hoping for an opportunity to lead African Americans in a boycott of the Montgomery buses.

Spreading the Word

In order for a boycott to work, everyone has to take part. People in Montgomery had to be told. Not everybody had televisions and telephones in the 1950s, and so the quickest way to inform people of the boycott was by word of mouth.

The Women's Political Council, a group of professional black women in Montgomery, spread the word about the boycott. Its members worked late into the night getting the message out.

Martin Luther King, Jr. (1929–1968)

Martin Luther King, Jr., grew up in Atlanta, Georgia. Both his father and his mother's father were Baptist ministers, and King became a minister, too. He was pastor at a Baptist church in Montgomery when the bus boycott began. After the boycott, King was soon recognized nationally as leader of the African American civil rights movement. He led many nonviolent protests, including the March on Washington in 1963, a peaceful protest by over 200,000 people. King was awarded the Nobel Peace Prize in 1964 and continued to campaign against oppression, war, and poverty until he was murdered.

The Boycott Begins

Civil rights leaders wondered if the people of Montgomery would have the courage to boycott. They were not disappointed. On the morning of Monday, December 5, 1955, there were no black passengers on the Montgomery buses.

The afternoon of December 5, a meeting was held at Holt Street Baptist Church. A new organization called the Montgomery Improvement Association (MIA) was formed there. The person chosen to be the leader of this group was a twenty-six year old minister named Martin Luther King, Jr.

Negroes Have Rights, Too
"Negroes have rights, too, for if Negroes did not ride the buses, they could not operate. If we do not do something to stop these arrests, they will continue. The next time it may be you, or your daughter, or mother."

Jo Ann Robinson, president of the Women's Political Council, in her flyer promoting the bus boycott, December 2, 1955

Martin Luther King worked hard to let people know what was happening in Montgomery and gain their support. This magazine published an article he wrote about the boycott.

APRIL 1956

an independent monthly

Liberation

Montgomery, Alabama:

OUR STRUGGLE

Martin Luther King

Articles by

Robert Granat   Sidney Lens   Bayard Rustin
Don Calhoun   George Woodcock

Volume I Number 2   30c

We Are Tired

"We are here this evening to say to those who have mistreated us so long that we are tired—tired of being segregated and humiliated, tired of being kicked about by the brutal feet of oppression."

*Martin Luther King, Jr.,
December 5, 1955*

Three Demands

At the meeting, it was decided that the boycott would continue until three changes were made in the bus system. First, black people wanted to be treated with respect on the buses. Second, blacks would not be forced to give up their seats for white passengers. Third, blacks would be hired as bus drivers.

Officials Fight the Boycott

On December 8, King and other members of the MIA presented their demands to city and bus company officials. They were turned down. In the coming months, the bus company and the government of Montgomery tried a number of ways to end the boycott.

The city fined black cab drivers who took people to work without charging the full fare. White women who drove their black maids to and from work were arrested for speeding. Black people who walked to work were arrested for loitering, or hanging around.

City officials also tried to trick the black community into thinking the boycott had ended. They told the local newspaper that the boycott was over. But everyone was quickly informed that the boycott was still on.

In February 1956, the city arrested about ninety people, including King, for activities related to the boycott. But this just called more attention to the protest, and the boycott in Montgomery gained support around the country.

The MIA bought station wagons, known as "rolling churches," that became taxis for boycotters. The Holt Street Baptist Church station wagon is now on display in the Rosa Parks Museum.

The task of the Supreme Court is to make sure U.S. laws comply with the Constitution. The Supreme Court justices hear about two hundred cases a year and make their decisions by a majority vote.

No Victory Allowed

"If we granted the Negroes these demands, they would go about boasting of a victory that they had won over the white people, and this we will not stand for."

Montgomery City Commissioner Clyde Sellers

Victories in Court

The bus company and city officials were determined not to give in. So in February 1956, the MIA went to court. Their **lawsuit** charged that bus segregation was unconstitutional. On June 4, the **federal** District Court ruled in favor of the MIA. The city of Montgomery refused to accept the decision, however, and appealed to the Supreme Court.

On November 13, 1956, the Supreme Court also ruled in favor of the MIA. The decision of the court was that segregation on buses was unconstitutional. Black people in Montgomery were delighted. They cried and hugged and cheered. The evening of November 13, a celebration was held at Holt Street Baptist Church. King delivered a stirring speech, saying, "We must not take this as a victory over the white man but as a victory for justice and democracy."

The End of the Boycott

The boycott lasted a few more weeks, until an official document confirmed the Supreme Court ruling. On December 21, 1956, Nixon, King, and other MIA members boarded a Montgomery bus. Rosa Parks also took her first bus ride in over a year. When Parks sat down this time, she could sit where she chose.

On December 21, 1956, the boycott was over. Martin Luther King took a seat on a Montgomery bus next to Glenn Smiley, a white minister from Texas.

A Remarkable Achievement

"The bus protest carried on by the colored people of Montgomery, Alabama, without violence, has been one of the most remarkable achievements of people fighting for their own rights, but doing so without bloodshed and with the most remarkable restraint and discipline, that we have ever witnessed in this country."

Eleanor Roosevelt, civil rights campaigner and widow of President Franklin D. Roosevelt

Chapter Four

Civil Rights

The Civil Rights Movement

Many white Southerners were angry about the Supreme Court's decision. They could not accept the idea of racial equality. But the Supreme Court's ruling had made history. The success of the boycott was the start of a civil rights movement that would transform the entire nation. From about 1955 to 1965, blacks and whites worked together in a variety of ways to bring an end to segregation.

The Little Rock Nine

Little Rock Central High School was supposed to be fully **integrated** at the start of school in September 1957. However, Arkansas's governor, Orval Faubus, tried to stop nine black children due to start at Central High from entering the building. The governor's racist action was stopped by President Dwight D. Eisenhower, who sent federal troops to escort the "Little Rock Nine" to school.

Little Rock student Elizabeth Eckford walks to school while white citizens of Little Rock pursue her and shout abuse.

Students in Greensboro, North Carolina, stage a sit-in at a whites-only lunch counter in 1960. They were making a peaceful protest against segregation.

Peaceful Protests

People were eager to get involved in the civil rights movement. The early protests were aimed at ending segregation of public facilities. Students staged **sit-ins** in public places, such as restaurants, where segregation was still practiced. Others, who called themselves "Freedom Riders," rode on segregated buses to protest at bus company rules.

In 1963, civil rights leaders decided to organize a march to Washington, D.C., to support a new civil rights law. This new law would ban racial **discrimination** in public places and encourage equal opportunities in employment and education. More than 200,000 people joined the march to the nation's capital on August 28, 1963.

One Man's Dream

"I have a dream that one day this nation will rise up, live out the true meaning of its creed: 'We hold these truths to be self-evident, that all men are created equal.' I have a dream that one day on the red hills of Georgia sons of former slaves and the sons of former slaveowners will be able to sit down together at the table of brotherhood. . . . I have a dream that my four little children will one day live in a nation where they will not be judged by the color of their skin but by the content of their character."

Martin Luther King, Jr., March on Washington, August 28, 1963

On July 2, 1964, President Lyndon Johnson signed the Civil Rights Act in a room filled with government and civil rights leaders. Still, African Americans in the South were prevented from voting.

Voting Rights

The Civil Rights Act was signed by President Lyndon Johnson on July 2, 1964. By this time, the civil rights movement had achieved a great deal. In the South, however, there were still laws making it difficult for black people to register as voters. Because of this, many African Americans were not voting. This meant they had no say in who represented them in government. As the civil rights movement progressed, it turned its attention to helping black people exercise their right to vote.

In the spring of 1965, a huge demonstration in favor of voting rights for black people was held in Selma, Alabama. On March 25, a crowd of about 25,000 people marched from Selma to Montgomery. Even Rosa Parks was there.

The protests about voting rights gained the support of the public. On August 6, 1965, President Johnson signed the Voting Rights Act. The law guarantees everyone's right to vote, regardless of color or race.

Affirmative Action

The civil rights movement had changed the laws that caused racial inequality in the United States. But people are not just segregated by laws. They are segregated by racist attitudes, by poverty, by lack of opportunity, and by where they live.

In the 1960s and 1970s, the government tried to create more opportunities for black people with **affirmative action**. This meant transporting students to schools outside of their neighborhoods so that schools became racially mixed. It also meant telling employers they had to hire qualified **minority** employees.

Some people argue that affirmative action discriminates against those who are not part of a minority. Others believe affirmative action is needed until everyone in society has equal opportunities.

Thousands of people gathered at the State Capitol building in Montgomery in 1965. They had marched there from Selma, Alabama. The Confederate flag, an old symbol of support for slavery from Civil War days, flies under the state flag on the Capitol dome.

Conclusion

The Lorraine Motel in Memphis, Tennessee, site of Martin Luther King's murder, is now the National Civil Rights Museum. King was shot when he stepped onto the motel balcony.

Free at Last
"…all God's children, black men and white men, Jews and gentiles, Protestants and Catholics, will be able to join hands and sing in the words of the old Negro spiritual: 'Free at last. Free at last. Thank God Almighty, we are free at last.'"

Martin Luther King, Jr., August 28, 1963, speaking in support of the Civil Rights Act

Honoring the Civil Rights Heroes

Martin Luther King, Jr., was assassinated on April 4, 1968, but his powerful **legacy** lives on. Martin Luther King, Jr. Day is celebrated every January on the Monday nearest his birthday on January 15.

To honor everyone else who has fought for African-American civil rights, Black History Month is celebrated in February each year. That month was chosen because important events in black history have taken place in February.

Rosa Parks

On December 1, 2000, forty-five years after the Montgomery bus boycott, Troy State University in Montgomery opened the Rosa Parks Library and Museum. The museum tells the story of the Montgomery bus boycott and ensures that Parks's memory will live on.

Rosa Parks, ninety years old in 2003, has received many honors and awards. She was given the NAACP's Spingarn Medal in 1970, the Martin Luther King, Jr. Award in 1980, and the Presidential Medal of Freedom in 1996. On June 15, 1999, Parks was awarded the Congressional Medal of Honor. During her speech, Parks said, "This medal is encouragement for all of us to continue until all have rights."

Inequality Continues

What did Rosa Parks mean by that? Maybe she meant that true equality has still not been reached. In spite of the civil rights movement and affirmative action, African Americans and other minority groups are generally still poorer than white people. White people continue to dominate national politics and other areas of influence in the United States.

Rosa Parks was sitting at the front of the black people's section on this bus when she refused to give up her seat in December 1955. The bus is now in the Henry Ford Museum.

Time Line

1619	First Africans are brought to America and sold as slaves.
1641	Massachusetts recognizes slavery as a legal institution.
1860	Abraham Lincoln is elected president.
1861	February: Confederate States of America is formed.
	April 12: Civil War begins.
1863	January 1: Emancipation Proclamation goes into effect.
1865	April 9: Confederate surrender ends Civil War.
	December 18: Thirteenth Amendment is approved.
1896	Supreme Court rules that segregation is acceptable.
1909	February: NAACP is founded.
1913	February 4: Birth of Rosa (McCauley) Parks.
1929	January 15: Birth of Martin Luther King, Jr.
1954	Supreme Court rules that segregation in schools is unlawful.
1955	August: Murder of Emmett Till.
	December 1: Rosa Parks refuses to give up her bus seat.
	December 5: Montgomery bus boycott begins.
1956	November 13: Supreme Court outlaws segregation on buses.
	December 21: Montgomery bus boycott ends.
1957	September: Integration of Little Rock Central High School.
1960	February 1: First sit-in takes place in Greensboro, North Carolina.
1961	May 4: Freedom rides to southern cities begin.
1963	August 28: March on Washington.
1964	July 2: Civil Rights Act is signed.
1965	March 25: Protest march from Selma, Alabama, reaches Montgomery.
	August 6: Voting Rights Act is signed.
1967	Thurgood Marshall is appointed as first black Supreme Court justice.
1968	April 4: Assassination of Martin Luther King, Jr.
1999	June 15: Rosa Parks receives Congressional Gold Medal of Honor.
2000	December 1: Rosa Parks Library and Museum opens in Montgomery.

Things to Think About and Do

Slavery and Segregation

Find out what you can about life as a slave in the United States in the 1700s and 1800s. Then think about what life was like for Africans Americans who lived under segregation. Compare those ways of life to that of a free citizen today. Make a list of the differences among the three types of existence.

Attitudes

Your grandparents were probably alive when segregation existed in the South. Talk to your grandparents or anyone else you know who was alive in the 1940s or 1950s. Ask them what they can remember about racial attitudes then. Were they aware of prejudice and did they experience segregation? Write down their answers and compare what they remember with attitudes today. What has changed? What is still the same?

Civil Rights

What do you think your civil rights are? Which are most important to you, and why? Write a couple of paragraphs about your civil rights and what makes them important.

Glossary

abolish:	get rid of or end.
activist:	person who takes action over issues in his or her society.
affirmative action:	action taken to make up for inequality in society.
Amendment:	official change or addition made to the United States Constitution.
boycott:	refusal to do business with a particular person or business.
civil rights:	basic rights—such as choice of religion—of every person.
civil war:	war between two groups in the same country.
desegregation:	getting rid of segregation.
discrimination:	showing preference for one thing over another. Racial discrimination happens when one racial group is given preference over another racial group.
economy:	system of producing and distributing goods and services.
emancipation:	freeing of African Americans and others held as slaves.
federal:	having to do with the whole nation rather than separate states.
figurehead:	person who acts as a good example rather than an actual leader.
integrated:	mixed together, as when schools were desegregated.
lawsuit:	case brought before a court of law for decision.
legacy:	something left behind for future generations.
minority:	of smaller number, such as African Americans in a society where more people, or the majority, are white.
oppression:	keeping down of one group or person by another group or person.
racist:	having opinions about a person based on race rather than on true qualities.
segregation:	separation of people of different races.
sit-in:	protest in which people sit down and refuse to move.
Supreme Court:	highest court in the United States.
unconstitutional:	action or law that goes against the U.S. Constitution.

Further Information

Books

Benjamin, Anne. *Young Rosa Parks: Civil Rights Heroine* (First-Start Biographies). Troll, 1996.

Haskins, James. *The Freedom Rides*. Hyperion Press, 1995.

Levine, Ellen. *If You Lived at the Time of Martin Luther King*. Scholastic, 1994.

Stein, R. Conrad. *Cornerstones of Freedom: The Montgomery Bus Boycott*. Children's Press, 1993.

Welch, Catherine A. *Children of the Civil Rights Era* (Picture the American Past). Carolrhoda Books, 2001.

Web Sites

www.ferris.edu/jimcrow/menu.htm The Jim Crow Museum at Ferris State University seeks to explain racism and racial stereotyping through its online exhibition.

www.tsum.edu/museum The Rosa Parks Museum and Library at Troy State University in Montgomery has online exhibit about the Montgomery Bus Boycott and lots of information about Rosa Parks and her achievements.

www.naacp.org The web site of the National Association for the Advancement of Colored People offers historical information and current news about African-American civil rights.

Useful Addresses

Rosa Parks Library and Museum
251 Montgomery Street
Montgomery, AL 36104
Telephone: (334) 241-8615

Index

Page numbers in **bold** indicate pictures.